Make It BIG

I0427534

By

Frank Figliomeni

Make it Big   Frank Figlomeni

Table of Contents

Make it Big   Frank Figlomeni

Introduction

This is dedicated to all those people who are striving to the goal of being financially successful.

This will provide you the understanding on how to increase your finances in order meet your financial goal of what you determine is 'success'.

This is not a get rich scheme or scam to give you delusions that if you following a few simple tricks then suddenly you will be rich. If you want a quick and easy guide to being rich I need to let you know it does not exist.

Wealth is built with some fundamental steps that can increase your goal of being rich.

If all you are willing to do is drink beer and watch TV or stay on the computer watching videos this is not for you.

You will need to do work hard and at times it can be difficult. You will need to look for ways to increase your income and reduce your debt.

Learn how to provide a service and add value to others and reap the benefits of your hard work.

If you persevere you can reap a better financial future and take the road that could lead you on the millionaire road to success.

Be sure to consult a lawyer and financial adviser as all countries do not have the same laws which you will need to understand in making certain decisions.

Let us start this journey to get you going on your way to success.

I Want Money

Money, money, money - I want lots of money. Join the club because you and most everyone else want lots of money so they can get out of the 'RAT RACE' and enjoy their lives in luxury. The world revolves around money with the haves and has not.

You want to be one of the 'have a lot'!

Well good for you as many people say they want lots of money yet settle for a job 9 to 5 with limited income. Before I show you how to make lots of money let us begin with understanding exactly what is money. Let us begin your financial journey by getting to understand the main source to being financial successful which is money.

To begin let me give you a brief overview of how money came into being.

Today money is what all people in society need in order to exchange goods or services.

In the past (thousands of years ago) there was no money so people used the barter system. The barter system is basically when one person exchanges what one person possesses (or can do) in exchange for something that someone possesses (or can do in return).

An example would be if John has many chickens yet has no goats. At this point in time money does not exist so how does John get a goat? The solution was that John who wants to have a goat goes to Bob who has several goats yet no chickens. Bob may have chickens yet he may want some more chickens.

John goes to Bob and after some negotiating they agree to an exchange of four chickens for a goat. John gives the four chickens to Bob and Bob gives John the goat which was agreed upon.

At the beginning of our history that is how it was done.

It became inconvenient to walk around with goats, chickens or whatever which were large and difficult to transport. As time passed the barter system was reduced by what people crave more which was silver and gold. These metals - gold and silver - still have financial value today.

Money was in coins made with gold silver or other minerals which were minted with the country's political leaders figure example Roman emperor.

As time progressed paper money was introduced which was backed by gold of that country. Paper money was not accepted at first as people were accustomed to using coins which were made of silver or gold.

As time passed paper money become the norm as it held value due to gold which that country owned that backed up the paper giving it value.

In the 1970's in the USA the gold backing for paper money was moved and replaced by oil backing the dollar. The petro-dollar was born.

The next step currently in some countries is that the paper money is only guaranteed by that government. If the government fails (economic collapse) then the money has no value anymore.

Today we are undergoing the next possible stage for currencies which is Bitcoin and crypto currencies. Since this is relatively new most people are wary of these currencies yet bit by bit people are slowly beginning to accept the currency.

Some countries are accepting this new currency which will make it more acceptable to people to accept.

Time will tell whether it is fully accepted by the masses.

Why you need Money

The reason you and I need money is to survive.

You need money to pay for shelter, food, and clothing - the basics of life. In short you need money to pay the bills and live comfortably.

If you have excess amounts of money you can live in luxury and that is what we all strive to obtain.

There are some people who will say that money is not everything and that is true yet if you do not have any money you better get used to living on the street. Without money you cannot take care of the basics of life or the luxuries of life such as taking a vacation.

Since you are reading this book I take it you understand what I just stated and have a desire to be wealthy. You must have some money or could not purchase this book.

With more money you can go from using the bus to owning your own car or if you have a car to getting a better one. You can get a better house, wardrobe, take vacations and other material possessions.

One reason you purchased this book was to learn how to increase your wealth - you want more money to enjoy the better things in life. You want a house or a bigger house, a luxury car, ability to take vacations when you want to go wherever you want.

If you have money you can support local charities.

The main point is it is better to have more money than to have less money. The worst is to have no money at all.

When to Start

The best time to start build your wealth is when you are young and the younger the better. In today's society most of the young people have little understanding of wealth building and are more concerned with enjoyment.

Many young boys and girls (men and women) will spend money that they do have on self indulgence. For example, video games, video consoles, shoes, large amounts of clothing, toys, partying and other items.

If you were to tell them to save money or to invest money they had received whether through gifts, part time jobs etc. they will look at you strange. The mindset of today is live for today and enjoys your life now.

This is the consumer mentality to spend, spend and spend and you will be happy.

THIS IS A TOTAL LIE!!

The Western Society is consumer based and it encourages the citizens to spend money on entertainment, personal products etc. This keeps the economy growing as more money spent means jobs are required which makes it good for business.

There is nothing wrong with spending some money for yourself - you do not want to be a miser wearing one set of clothes. You must start looking at a means to use some of the money you have to increase your wealth and avoid getting into bad debt. Some debt is good but more on that later.

The sooner you start the better to understanding compound interest. To increase wealth you must learn compound interest and use it to your advantage.

Money used properly can make you incredible rich.

Even a penny if you double it daily in 30 days would make you a millionaire.

Here is the sample.

Day 1: $.01
Day 2: $.02
Day 3: $.04
Day 4: $.08
Day 5: $.16
Day 6: $.32
Day 7: $.64
Day 8: $1.28
Day 9: $2.56
Day 10: $5.12
Day 11: $10.24
Day 12: $20.48
Day 13: $40.96
Day 14: $81.92
Day 15: $163.84
Day 16: $327.68
Day 17: $655.36
Day 18: $1,310.72
Day 19: $2,621.44
Day 20: $5,242.88
Day 21: $10,485.76

Day 22: $20,971.52
Day 23: $41,943.04
Day 24: $83,886.08
Day 25: $167,772.16
Day 26: $335,544.32
Day 27: $671,088.64
Day 28: $1,342,177.28
Day 29: $2,684,354.56
Day 30: $5,368,709.12

In thirty days you are a millionaire just by doubling a penny. You need to learn to use all available money to work for you and create more money.

The Winning Attitude

In order to be successful in finance you will need to have a certain mindset. I have listed those which I believe are the main mindset to get what you want in life.

Get a Positive Attitude

In order to get what you want you have to believe you will achieve your goal. Being positive will carry you during the times when things get rough in your endure for success.

Most people stop going for their goals because they lack a positive attitude. When things get off track on the road to achieving the goal they let fear take over and then stop going for the goal.

I can't express how much having a positive attitude is necessary to achieve the goal in anything in life. Many rich people failed time and time again yet they had a positive attitude and persevered until finally they reached the goal.

Always remember if it was easy then everyone would be rich.

Most people take the easy road in life and lead a simple, poor or middle class life. If you want to make it big you have to be able to handle the rough times and rejection.

The people around you both family and friends may try to advise you to stop what you are doing and take the safe road - a good job. They will mean well in their intentions and looking to protect you from failure yet they are actually preventing you from your success.

This is why you need a positive attitude to succeed.

Use Time Effectively

Plan your daily activities in order to maximize your chances to achieve your goal. If you do not have a plan then you will be all over the place and wasting time in many meaningless and unimportant tasks.

Reduce watching television and using other social media unless it brings you closer to your goal.

Stop wasting time on daily time wasters such as people who waste your time on gossip and meaningless nonsense. What they say may be interesting or not yet if it is not bringing you closer to your goal it is a waste of time.

Get yourself a small blank notepad or free online application and make a schedule to track how you spend your day. You will see how you spend your day and I am certain you will be amazed how much time you waste. You are precious and so is your time.

Stop wasting your time!

Upgrade your skills and network.

In this day and age it is easy to be replaced by someone else in your current job. There is always someone who is looking to take your place at work. The higher you are in a company the more people below you want your job as it is higher paying with more perks.

The business politics gets worse the higher you are in any company so you must always be aware of what is going on in order to act accordingly to keep your job.

If you currently have a company and your company does the same thing over and over then others will soon pass you by. You need to be aware of the competition, what is new and how it may affect you and your business.

You need to join groups which deal in the same field you are interested in order to achieve your goal. If you want to be rich then join groups which deal with the subject of wealth creation.

Join organizations regarding how to invest, making money in real estate, business start ups and other such type of groups. They can be found online by doing a search.

Remember to do your homework as there are money scams out there eager to take your money. Your goal is to increase your wealth not lose it by getting scammed.

Beware!

Education does not stop at end of high school or college. The wealthy people will tell you that their smarts came not from school rather from learning from other people who made it big.

The current school system is designed to give you basic understanding so you can read, write and do some math. It does not teach you how to create wealth. School teaches you how to get a job in a specific field.

Depending on the field you choose the pay can be good yet you will not be making millions of dollars. The exception to this rule in order to be a millionaire is an employee who moves up in company and after many years (maybe 20 or 30 years) becomes CEO of a major company.

Guess what, your life is almost over and do you really want to wait until you are over fifty to 'maybe' become rich. Remember that only a handful of people become leaders of large companies.

If you do want to take that chance and prefer to move up in the company then take all the courses you can to improve your skills to enable you to be valuable and move up the ladder.

Note: Just keep in mind that the odds are against you and many end up old with a pension never reaching great wealth. They will end up with an average or below average income having to be careful what they purchase. You purchased this book in order to be a millionaire so that is not the road you want to take. Let us look at the millionaire road.

If you decide you do not want to wait to move up the ladder then you will need to look at starting a business for yourself and investments. This is the millionaire road.

On this road you need to improve your business skills and inter-personnel skills. Take course and join some groups to improve your skills. Read books by people who made it rich and see what they did and duplicate the action and avoid what they avoided.

You must use some common sense and it is possible you may have to adjust your actions as required as everyone is different and times and situations can change quickly.

Find yourself a mentor who is already successful in the field you want to get involved with and learn all you can from that person. Take the person out for a coffee or lunch and learn as much as you can.

This works best if you can build a friendship with the person and they are more willing to share information and help and guide you with their expertise.

What do I do now?

Everyone is different and the values will vary person from person. You must start your journey to wealth creation with the end in mind. You must set for yourself a **goal** and determine when you want that goal to be reached.

Ask yourself these questions and answer them before you move forward:

How much wealth do I want to make me happy and comfortable?

When do I want to reach my goal?

	Where skills do I currently have now to help me reach my goal?
1	
2	
3	
4	

	Where skills do I need to help me reach my goal?
1	
2	
3	
4	

How do I get the skills that I currently lack?	
1	
2	
3	
4	

When will I be able to get the appropriate skills?	
1	
2	
3	
4	

What groups do I need to join to reach my goals?
1
2
3
4

Our society is based in instant self gratification and many people will spend money on frivolous items to provide a momentary gratification.

In order to build wealth then you must have a plan in place and start working on it to obtain your goal.

Do not keep your plan as an idea rather put it on paper and remind yourself daily of what your goal is and start putting your plan into action.

How to Build Wealth

In order to build wealth you need to have some money in order for it to grow. Unless you are born a prince/princess or have inherited millions then you like most of us need to start making money prior to increasing your wealth.

The first method which you should NOT do is to engage in illegal activities such as selling drugs, armed robber etc.

Do not do these activities.

Now to the law abiding ways to make and build wealth.

Get some Money

The most common method to start making money is you need to get some type of job. When you are in high school try getting a part-time job in order to make some money.

For those who are in school or out of school the following applies to get a job.

Get a resume setup and check for spelling. Send it to all the companies in your area and go in person if you can. Some companies prefer to see you in person as they receive multitudes of resumes and it is easy to be just another name on a list.

You need to stand out from others and going in person makes you stand out. For more professional positions you cannot go in person yet if you can contact the hiring manager via phone or email that is a plus on your side.

Make sure for the interview that you are well dressed and clean to improve your chances of getting that position. If you are dressed looking like a slob then you will definitely decrease your chance of getting that position.

Before you go to the interview be prepared by learning what the company does and know about the position you applied.

During the interviewer use a firm hand shake. You should present yourself as confident and make the interviewer know ways ***you can help the company***.

Remember it is not about you rather it is about how you can help the company that will get you the job. At the end either you will be offered job on the spot or if not, ask what the next steps in the hiring process. You want to know when he or she will determine who will be hired.

Send a follow up email thanking the interviewer for the time spent and again restate your interest in the position. This is to make you stand out and give you a greater chance to get that position.

Be the Boss

You now have some money and you either still work at the company or break all ties and be your own boss.

The benefit to having a job is that it provides a certain income. You get either an hourly rate or a salary for your time. The problem is it limits you to a certain amount of money you can make.

There are some drawbacks to a job such as the illusion that you have a steady pay cheque. Notice I said illusion as you can be terminated from your position at anytime. The company can decide to downsize and suddenly you have no position.

You may be or know someone who went to work and gets called into the bosses office and human resources is present. They are given their walking papers. This is hard to grasp yet a job is not forever. Most people fall into that illusion and live their life as if they will always be working at their position.

Some people do keep the job until retirement yet end up with a small pension but never make it rich.

If you decide to stay at a job just understand that you are limiting yourself to a specific income which can end suddenly.

If you want to give yourself the option of unlimited income then you will need to move to another way of thinking and working.

The higher the risk you are willing to take the greater the return. Before you venture to start a business you should assess if you have what it takes as some people are content to just work at a job - 9 to 5 and get a steady pay cheque.

One way to give yourself the chance for higher income is to be your own boss either full-time or a more cautious method via a part-time business. In order to increase your wealth then you need to look at getting another job or being your own boss.

You want to be a millionaire so you have to transition from employee to being the boss. It will not be easy to accomplish yet others have done it and so can you.

Some Business Types

There are many types of business you can start such as gardener, accounting, pet groomer, technical specialist and more. The business types are almost endless but before you start anything you need to understand the business structure best suited for you to start.

Let us start with the first type of business structure which is called **Sole Ownership**. In this type of business you are the sole owner of the company. You are the one who makes all the decisions and take all the benefits and liabilities which are incurred.

Let me break this done with the pros and cons of this type of business model.

Pros:

1. You are the only owner and do not have to deal with another person to make decisions.
2. You get to choose when to work and how long you want to work.
3. You do not have to ask to take time off.
4. You get all the financial benefits and do not need to share with anyone except government regarding taxes).
5. You can change company direction at any time - flexible environment.

Those are some of the benefits to going sole proprietor route yet there is the down side **(cons)** to this which is as follows.

Cons:

1. You are responsible if anything happens 'personally' due to the company actions. For example, if you do a job which has issues you can be sued by the other party who you did work. They can go after the assets and also your personal assets. Note: Millionaires never take this route as it leaves them open to total financial disaster. You can lose your life savings if something happens since you are held accountable.

2. If you do not choose to work you will not make any money. You are the company and income is obtained only if and when you are working.

3. Health benefits are costly and you have to cover this yourself. If you are seriously ill you have no income to cover you and you can end up losing your business and/or your house.

4. You are limited to what you know and can learn. There is no one to back you up if something happens.

5. Funding to keep business going comes from you alone unless a friend or family will lend you money.

Proprietorship (Partnership)

This type of business structure is when two or more people own one business. This is a slightly different from sole proprietorship. This model also has its pros and cons.

Pros:

1. You have someone helping grow the business and greater chance to grow the business.
2. If you are off the business can still run as the partner can step in.
3. You can bounce ideas of someone else and avoid some business mistakes.
4. More income can be raised by two or more people to grow business.
5. Should there by a downturn in business more funds available to get through the bad times.

Cons:

1. You need to both agree for a decision to be made regarding business direction.
2. One partner may have a different direction for the company which can lead to arguments and stressful situations.
3. You are legally responsible for your partners conduct. If the partner does something that is illegal or damaging (business related) then you are also accountable and can be sued. For example your partner takes all the business cash and leaves the country. You are held accountable to meet your client responsibilities and can be sued if you do not meet the client obligation (contract). **Note:** You also got robbed by your partner and that hurts.

Many people decide against this due to the exposure you have to being sued and losing everything. To be a millionaire I suggest you avoid this business structure.

Corporation or Incorporation

Most people decide to start a company by incorporating the business and this insulates the owner from personal legal liabilities. There may be some situations which they are legally liable yet that would have to be deliberate fraud by owner.

Here are some benefits (pros) to incorporating.

Pro:

1. By incorporating you and the company are two separate entities. If someone sues the company for any reason then they can go only against the company assets yet not after your own personally assets.
2. In the event the company goes bankrupt for whatever reason then you are not affected as you are a separate entity. Your personal assets are protected.
3. A company name is more professional and appealing to clients. People have more confidence in a corporation instead of a one man or women operation.

4. You can write-off expenses such as car, truck, gas, insurance, furniture and more. Discuss with your accountant regarding all write-offs for your business.

Cons:

1. The cons are the additional cost to incorporate. You need to spend money to get yourself incorporated yet it is a benefit as it protects you from personal liability.
2. You must collect taxes for work done and report on a regular basis - additional cost.

Business Accounting

You will need to understand some business concepts such as accounting. In order to move forward you must understand assets, liabilities, expenses, income, (ROI) return on investment, cash flow and more.

Let us start with understanding what is an asset?

An asset can be defined as a useful or desirable quality.

In general terms something you own and benefit from is considered an asset. If you own a car it is considered an asset as is a house. A computer is an asset and a television is an asset. If you own a business the good will of your company is considered an asset. If you have rights to copyrighted material, patents or own a trademark these are also considered assets.

Assets are both tangible as seen in car ownership and intangible as seen in a company's good will.

We are conditioned to obtain assets by the media, our parents and society in general.

Having assets makes you a wealthy person.

Having a house is an asset but if the mortgage is greater than the house price then it is a bad asset.

The people who lost their houses during the recession in 2008 would agree. When you sell your house you need someone to buy it for more than you paid that is true yet if the market falls you may have no buyers. The mortgage payment, taxes and utilities to maintain the house then can be viewed as liabilities.

In regards to wealth creation I would define some assets as an investment or any item which generates an income giving a positive cash flow. Renting part or the entire house then makes it an asset with positive cash flow.

Should you decide to purchase a house you may look at renting part of the house. The renter who pays you will offset your costs and by giving a positive cash flow can decrease the time to pay off the mortgage on the house.

Here is an simple example:

Monthly Cost

Mortgage	$ 1,200.00
Land Tax	$ 300.00
Utilities	$ 300.00
Total Cost	**$ 1,800.00**

Monthly Income

Renter 1	$ 950.00
Renter 2	$ 950.00
Total Income	$1,900.00

Positive Income $ 100.00 monthly

In this example you are living free and making $100.00 every month. Based on your personal cost and rental costs in your area this will change yet you get the idea.

You need a renter to cover your costs if possible or at least reduce your costs which gives you more free money in order to invest.

What is a Liability?

A liability is a good or service you must pay for in accounting.

Many people are conditioned very young to get a good education and then a get a good paying job with growth potential. After this then society says buy a new car and take vacations. The only problem with this situation is although it may feed your ego and make you happy at first; there is still the matter of the debt you now have to pay off. .

By putting yourself in debt you will now have a difficult time getting out of that debt and little chance of creating wealth. You need to get out of personal debt in order to create wealth.

Debt that is used to create wealth is different and I will address that later.

Personal debt is a great enemy and must be overcome. You need to check your purchases and not be overly self indulgent in your spending.

If you spend on items which may create wealth then this is good - such as an education. The money you spend to educate yourself will increase potential for wealth creation yet you need to get rid of that loan ASAP.

Personal debt (bad debt) for example, a new car is a major liability.   A car is an expense and an asset. You need to pay a monthly fee to pay off the loan or pay for the rental of the car. You need to pay the car insurance and then the gas to get you around in the car. Then you must pay for general maintenance and car repairs when it breaks down. Notice how much money is being spent to own and maintain the car.

If you really need a car I suggest you get yourself a solid used car and let someone else lose the 30% on the new car purchase. I believe a car depreciates 30% once driven off the lot - maybe more or less.

When you want to sell the car you never get your money back as it depreciates. A car is a luxury item and in most cases guaranteed to lose you money.

Now let us look back at home ownership. This can be a liability or an asset. You do need to live somewhere so some money will go out from your pocket. A house needs you to cover the mortgage payments, taxes, utilities and then general repairs or any upgrades.

Renting may be a better option yet renting is making someone else rich. Renting or owning a home and living by you is a liability. Yet owning a home and renting part of the home is an asset.

If you buy a home then you can make it an asset by having part of it rented. If not rented a house is also viewed as a liability.

Other liabilities are when you purchase furniture on credit. The credit interest you pay is a liability but you get the idea.

Get Other Source of Income.

You should look at ways to create other sources of income. Other sources of income can be writing a book, music —teaching or creating songs, create a blog, selling products and more. There are other sources you can look into yet it is necessary to have other sources of income in order to be a millionaire.

In order to be wealthy you need more than one source of income to reach that goal or one very high source of income. It is time consuming and hard especially if you also have a full time job. Juggling a job and side business is hard to do yet you need to force yourself to see it through. Regardless of being hard you should look into other sources of income as it is necessary to make you wealthy.

The other reason is that if you lose your main income 'the job' you have another source of income so you will not be in a financial disaster. Losing a job will be less stressful as you are not dependant on that one source of income since you already have other sources of income.

Time and Money

One of the main concepts you need to understand and put into practice is to separate your time from money in order to be a millionaire. As long as you work for an hourly wage it is rare you will be extremely wealthy. The mega rich learned that you need to make money even while you sleep and not just based on time.

There is a progression that you should follow to reach this goal.

1. To start you need to leverage time for money via a job. You need to save some money that you can pay your bills to survive. After this point you need to have saved some money in order to start a side business.
2. The side (or full time) business is started and needs your time to get going. You are still trading time for money at this point.
3. Business is established with little time for you to just oversee. Others do most of the work and you make money on sales and their time. You make money even when you sleep.

The owners of giant retailers are multi-millionaires (billionaires?). They have their wealth not created by their time spent at work rather others do the work at stores, distribution centers, sales, marketing etc and they reap the benefits of the employees labour. Even in a business your time is money and you have only a certain amount of time in a day.

If you base your income only on time you are limiting your income.

For example let us say you are making $100.00 an hour. What would you have at the end of the year?

Hourly rate $ 100.00

8 hours $800.00

5 Days a week $ 4,000.00

52 weeks $ 208,000.00

Now remember you still have to pay taxes so let us remove 40% for taxes.

You are now left with $ 124,800.00.

That is a really good pay yet how many people make $100.00 an hour? Maybe some lawyers and doctors but that is not the wage of the average person.

You want to position yourself that your money is not tied into your time. Ever wonder why some musicians are so rich?

The reason is that their time is not tied to the hourly rate. When a musician makes a hit song he/she receives royalties based on the number of units sold. They also receive income for airplay on radio stations. While they are sleeping people all over the world are either buying or listening on the radio to their song and the musician gets money. What a life to do something once and get paid even when you are sleeping.

Let us take for example large store - I will not use a specific company. When people go the store and purchase products or services the owner is making money. You will notice that the wealth is not tied to the owner's time doing work rather on the item or service being sold.

Let us take for example YouTube where people of successful channels are paid royalties for the amount of views (ads) when there video is monetized.

Reduce your time for money in order to be rich!

Ways to Increase Your Wealth

How do you use your money?

In order to create wealth then does not follow what most people do which is to spend everything on their self indulgence. These people live pay cheque to pay cheque with little thought of tomorrow.

These people go out to eat at restaurants on a regular basis to enjoy the weekend. Some will buy cases of beer to get drunk and have fun on the weekend. They will spend large amounts of their pay cheque to enjoy themselves after a hard week of work.

Others also will spend large amounts of money on clothing - they latest style in order to be fashionable. Then there are others who spend large amounts on electronics such as the latest gadgets. They need to get it first to satisfy themselves. Then you have those who need the latest video game or video console and wait hours in line to get it.

There are many other ways which people like this spend most of their money yet the main takeaway is to understand their money is spent on self indulgences.

I understand you may want to get that new video game or new clothes, cologne or perfume and by all means do so as you only live once. My point is that you need to take a portion of what you make and put that away and do not touch that money.

If all you do is spend your money on self indulgence then how can you build wealth? If what you spend your money on can build wealth then great as you are on the right path, but not on excess items which do not build wealth.

In order to build wealth you need to save your money to be used on wealth building items.

Be the one who sells the items or services.

For now let us start with initial wealth building via savings.

You can start to save by using the 10% rule which states whatever you make you put the 10% gross aside in a saving account or some other type of investment. The investment should have a guarantee to protect your initial investment - money you put in. If you can put more money away than the 10% then I suggest you do so to speed up the wealth increase.

The more you put away and the younger your age the greater the return will be down the road.

Let us look at a savings account.

Savings

All banks and financial institutions will vary on the savings account details so you need to look and see the savings account that best suites you. One main benefit in savings is that for the most part the money is secure yet you may lose some money on monthly fees. You should get a savings account with no monthly fee - this depends on your banks policy

You should put at least 10% gross income from your earning into a savings account as soon as you are paid. If you can have a direct deposit to the account done by your employer even better as by not seeing that amount you will adjust your spending habits and not notice it being taken out of your pay.

With interest rates so low you will see little growth in the investment yet you need to start somewhere. After some time it will grow and then you can look at other investments to use that money.

Whatever you do you must avoid the temptation to use that sum which just grew on some personal none wealth building items, ex - new video system.

You need discipline in order to start being wealthy.

Ok, so now you have some money what do I do?

Well then you need wealth building items which can increase your wealth faster and there are many available. Let us look at a few beginning with stocks.

.

Stocks

A stock in a company is a unit of ownership in the company which it is purchased. This means when you buy a stock you are a part owner of the company. There are different types of stocks such as common shares or preferred shares which have different types of rules and limitations. Some stocks have dividends paid at certain times and amount per year for each share you hold while other have no dividends. I will not get too detailed on stock types except to state that you should look at shares what will pay dividends.

There are different types of stock, some 'blue chip' stocks which are large companies such as IBM which will most likely be around and not default. There are other types of stocks known as 'penny stocks' which have high volatility and you can make big gains or big losses. There are different types of stock to consider. Some stocks the wealth comes from capital gains and others also provide dividends.

Dividends are a percentage return based on number of stocks you hold and it varies for each type of stock. You need to get the details prior to purchasing the stock.

All stocks can increase in value per share and increase your money yet keep in mind that the stock can also go down and you can lose money.

You need to also take into account the administration cost. That means there is the cost for purchasing the stock or selling it pending which options is chosen.

Stock can make you really rich or can make you lose everything on a downturn. Be careful if investing in stocks and make sure you do your homework. Get as much information on the company and seek professional help on this one. You may need to get a broker or financial planner to see the impact of purchasing stock.

Remember that you never lose or win regarding stocks until you actually sell the stock share so timing is very important.

Mutual Funds

This method will allow more flexibility of choices. There are funds which are more for the conservative person which provide a guaranteed amount or at least will secure the original amount invested.

There are other funds which are more for the higher risk taker which provide a potential greater return yet have a chance for a greater lose if the fund tanks. These funds are more volatile. For mutual funds you need to discuss with a representative to determine your level of comfort.

My suggestion is that if you are young and at the start of a job/business then go for a more volatile fund. If you do lose then you have time to recover the money back.

If you are middle aged then I suggest a mix of volatile and conservation funds. You need to protect you income to a point yet you would need some funds to take a chance for greater return.

If you are looking at retiring or retired you should be heavily in conservative funds and guaranteed funds. At this point in your life you need to protect what you have earned as you do not have time to make up the money if it goes down.

This only drawback in protecting what you have puts you in a position which you are not investing and therefore how can you make it big?

The higher the risk means possible higher return or loses. The lower risk the chance of lower return and lose.

Real-estate

This is a very tricky one to deal with. In order to get into real-estate you usually need money for a down payment and have a job to show you can pay the mortgage.

This debt is good in the sense that the goal is to use the debt to create greater wealth. Buying a piece of land and selling it a few years later at a greater cost can increase your wealth. The risk is that if the land value goes down and this can happen. In this case you lose money if you need to sell so just be aware of this fact.

Do not fall for the scam that you always make money on real-estate.

Some people purchase a house to rent to others. They may live in part of it or rent the whole house. If you can get rental income that covers the mortgage and taxes and have the renter handle the utilities you make a positive cash flow. In time the house cost should usually go up yet it can decline - just be aware.

The other issue you need to deal with is problem renters which do not pay or damage your property. You may be stuck trying to get them out while they live at your house for free. Do you have enough money to cover the cost of a mortgage if they don't pay and the legal fees to evict the bad renters?

You should do a background check on the potential renters this may reduce the chance of getting a 'professional renter'.

Professional renters will rent houses or apartments and soon after will not pay the rent. They know the law and use it to live rent free for a period of time until they find another place to rent and do the same thing all over again. They will cost you plenty to get rid of them so be aware.

Should you however end up renting to a good tenant then you can cover the costs and make money which is your goal. Be aware of both sides to this endeavor.

Start a Business

In previous chapter I have defined the type of business structure you can begin. I recommend incorporating your business for reasons previously stated.

Protecting the Nest with Insurance

Insurance is important to secure your investments and life. If you are married you should have life insurance to protect your loved ones in case of your death. This is not a pleasant thing to address yet there is a reality - no one lives forever. You need to insure that your loved ones would be taken care of if you die - ex. car accident.

The amount of coverage depends on your situation in life - are you just married, one child or several children.

In this case you should discuss this with a life insurance agent to see what fits your current situation and how much coverage you need and can afford.

Debt Reduction

You need to get a handle on your debts. If you went to school and have a student loan then you should be aiming to eliminate that debt ASAP. The benefit of education should provide a higher paying position yet the debt with the interest you are paying is impacting the time it will take to create your wealth.

If you purchased a vehicle or some furniture on credit then you should be targeting to eliminate this debt by putting extra money on your payment to remove this debt.

You want to use interest in order grow your wealth and not having to pay extra interest for any item which makes someone else rich. By paying interest on an item you reduce your wealth and some rates for ex. furniture - the interest can be up to 18%. This may vary pending the financial market. Credit card payments are oer 20% which is a big hit to your financial plan.

It is easy to get seduced by using your credit card for impulse items. That new pair of shoes you just have to have or that new video game etc.

This purchase may give you immediate satisfaction yet you need to prioritize - do you need that item?

Taxes Deductions, Refunds and Coupons

In order to increase your wealth you should take advantage of tax deductions. When you are completing your taxes get all the deductions you can get for yourself. In Canada you can use RRSP's to reduce your taxes and possibly get a refund. In other countries there will be similar tax deductions you can use.

I suggest you get a professional accountant to have them review your taxes and provide you professional advice in order to reduce your taxes.

Another area you should use is coupons which can reduce your cost on regular daily items. Stores usually provide coupons and there are sites which provide a list of coupons and sales.

Check your weekly store flyer in order to take advantage of the sales on grocery or other personal items.

This is an excellent method to cut your costs on a regular bases. Try to avoid paying full price on items as most items at one point may go on sale.

I have heard of cases in which people have saved thousands of dollars a year by using coupons. This is time consuming yet the savings may be worth the effort you put in.

Will

You should have a will drawn up by a lawyer to ensure that your assets are distributed to those you want in case of your death. I suggest you do not do this yourself and get it done by a lawyer who will provide guidance based on your current situation in life.

Your will should be reviewed ever several years or if they is a major change in your life circumstance. I know this will cost extra yet this will avoid much anguish to those left behind having to deal with your death.

Rules for Success

These are what I consider to be the major rules in order to be successful.

1) Define your goal.

Everyone has their own view of what financial success is to them.

Do you want to make a million dollars every year?

Do you want to be a multi-millionaire in 2 years?

Whatever your goal is you need to define it in your mind and write it down. The reason you write down your goal is to keep it as a reminder because if you do not you will soon forget about it and it will be nothing more than a nice little dream.

You need to set goals and avoid the trap of just dreaming about a better future. When you set goals make sure that you make it as specific as possible. Put a time of when you want to reach the goal.

Ensure you have a method of how you will reach your goals. Make the goal you set for yourself to be attainable.

Here is a bad example of a goal.

'I want to be a millionaire'.

This goal has no time limit, method to attain and is just a dream.

Here is an example of a goal you can work towards.

'I want to make a million dollars in 5 years. I will setup a business in landscaping by purchasing used equipment such as a lawn mower, weed trimmer, shovels, and snow blower. I will do door to door in my area and reach out to companies in my area. I am targeting $100,000 in my first years with an aggressive marketing plan. This will expand to $200,000 in years two and $250,000 in year 3,4 and 5.'

This goal has details on HOW you will reach the financial goal. The timelines you will notice have been set for yourself which includes the strategy regarding marketing is discussed.

The goal you set for yourself will vary from my example yet keep the concept of detail, time and method in place.

2) Do not care what other people think of you.

You will notice very quickly that when you start taking action to move from your current position in life to a better one financially that people will try to tear you down. Family and friends will start to criticise what you are doing some out of concern that you may fail and try to save you from yourself.

Others will do this out of envy and jealousy because your desire to move up will make them have to look at themselves and they will not like what they see.

They will want to keep you down with them and you will start hearing some comments such as, 'you think you are better than me' or 'you think we are not good enough for you.'

This is to be expected as it happens all the time. I have had the personal experience when I was promoted to a high level in my job. My friends and people I hung out with suddenly changed attitude with me. Some stopped speaking to me and others kept the conversation formal and not casual. With my promotion I lost some friends yet gained other friends at the next level.

Some started talking behind my back and not kindly by saying I did not deserve the promotion and they did deserve the promotion.

Expect this when you start to move up from where you currently either socially or financially. Just remember not to listen to what they say or it will destroy you.

I moved up by my merit and deserved the promotion. Any benefits you get in life remember you deserved it and let no one bring you down,

3) Keep on reading.

READ, read and read. The move you know the greater are the chances that you will succeed. You will need to know what is going on in your field and what the potential future direction in your area is. You need to be on top of things in your area that you have decided to pursue.

Stop wasting your time on meaningless and unproductive leisure activities like always watching television or playing video games. You need to spend time learning your specialty and that takes time and effort on your part.

You need to read up on your field to ensure that you are prepared for any changes that will impact you as you pursue your goal.

For example, if you are going for an Information technology business and creating an application then you would need to ensure that the final solution will be accepted by the general public. You need to read articles and demographics to ensure you will connect with the target audience.

By increasing your knowledge via reading you will make an informed decision increasing the success rate of your endeavor.

4) Model success from others that have reached the goal you desire.

You do not need to create the wheel just create a better wheel. Look at people who have succeeded in the field you are looking to enter then duplicate what they did yet make it slightly different that it will be your own.

The reason you do this is because the steps they took for success worked so if you duplicate it then in theory you should meet the same success - maybe greater or less.

It would be foolish to take the advice of someone who has constantly failed in all his/her business ventures. Obviously what they did failed so if you do the same why would you think you will succeed?

Chances are you would fail just as they did. You could learn from what they did and avoid the same pitfalls.

5) Be competitive in your field.

In any venture you undertake make certain you do more than just enough to get ahead. Make yourself an expert in the field you undertake, a leader of the pack so to speak. In any field you place yourself you will earn more if you are ahead of the pack and evaluating what others are doing - and then do it better.

If you make yourself competitive in your field you will continue to strive while others are falling behind or out all together.

You would think that this would be obvious yet it is not the case. Many people will start a venture - company etc, and will do just the basics to get by. When they do not see the massive results they want they cannot understand why they are not succeeding.

You get what you put into any venture company. You want big gains then you need to have something that others do not have and be competitive with your competition.

For example:

If you decide to start a fast food pizza place you and the competition will have to offer delivery. To be more competitive you can offer free delivery or a free pizza if they do not receive the order within a certain time period. Let us say one hour or 1/2 hour.

Suddenly this makes you more competitive than your others since you have an offer which they do not provide. If they decide to follow suite then you need to offer something else to make your product more desirable than the competition.

6) Work hard yet smart at the same time.

Hard working does not mean you will get noticed and promoted to a better job with higher pay. You need to ensure that the right people with power and influence notice you and are on your side.

People who have a powerful work network are the ones who move up in the company.

If you are going into your own business you need to build a good strong network that can get you moving up fast. These people can guide you and help you avoid common pitfalls in building a strong business.

You need to prioritize what is important and needs to be done and what is less important and may be done later or not at all.

7) Listen to people's advice yet make up your own mind to a decision.

You will get advice from many people but you will need to filter out the nonsense and keep what will assist you on your goal.

Some people will discourage you on your mission due to many reasons of their own such as jealousy, envy or hidden dislike of you and hoping you fail.

When you listen to people use reason and common sense to assist you on your decisions. You may fail at times due to taking bad advice or your own decisions yet remember to pick yourself up, regroup and try a different route.

8) Start small and grow big.

Unless you are born in a rich family with a striving business you will probably need to start small. Create a plan on what business or career you want to start. You may have little funds and will need to create an income flow via a job or business.

If starting a business start small and get knowledge on how it works, the pitfalls, means to increase wealth and reduce debt. This will take time and hard work but the rewards when achieved are with the labour.

9) Many income streams.

It is always a good idea to have more than one income stream. If one income stream dries up you have the other ones to lean on and can improve that lost stream or create another income stream.

The danger of many income streams is you need to keep an eye on all of them and you can lose track of some which will produce failure.

Have multiple income streams but only as much that you can handle.

Some income streams you can start are:

1. You tube channel
2. Influencer
3. Dog walker
4. House sitter
5. Sell old clothes
6. Create a blog
7. Take online surveys

The Plan

Many people read a book and then soon forget what they learned and go back to their old habits. The first step to financial success is to complete this section.

Answer the following question and keep as a reminder to reinforce and remind you daily of your commitment to succeed.

You get in life what you put in!

Why do I want to be Wealthy?

Write down the reasons you want to be wealthy to remind you daily and keep you on track.

1	
2	
3	
4	
5	
6	
7	
8	

What am I doing to meet my goal?

1	
2	
3	
4	
5	
6	
7	
8	

What are the benefits of me being wealthy?

1	
2	
3	
4	
5	
6	
7	
8	

What assets do I have to reach my goal?

1	
2	
3	
4	
5	
6	
7	
8	

What may be interfering with my goal?

1	
2	
3	
4	
5	
6	
7	
8	

How will I overcome these obstacles?

1	
2	
3	
4	
5	
6	
7	
8	

What have I done to correct any problems?

1	
2	
3	
4	
5	
6	
7	
8	

The Budget

The most common mistake people do is not to create a budget. In order to be financially fit you must know where all your money is going to whether mortgage payments, car payments, bills, personal expenses, luxury items, impulse buying etc.

Get yourself a small book to keep track of all the money you spend and review after a week. You will be shocked to see how much is spent on frivolous items yet adding up to a lot at the end of the week.

If you have a computer or tablet you can get a template or make one to keep track of your spending and investments. You will need to constantly review your spending habits, investments and personal goals or they will get out of control.

Investments need to be checked as there may be a better one yielding better returns. To be financially successful you need to be on top of things and not let other people take full control of your finances.

To help you out I added some pages at the end of this book so you can write in your daily expenses.

Remember your financial future is in your hands.

Expense Tracker

Date _____

I spent money on the following:

Item	My reason to purchase	Cost

Date _____

I spent money on the following:

Item	My reason to purchase	Cost

Date _____

I spent money on the following:

Item	My reason to purchase	Cost

Date _____

I spent money on the following:

Item	My reason to purchase	Cost

Date _____

I spent money on the following:

Item	My reason to purchase	Cost

Date _____

I spent money on the following:

Item	My reason to purchase	Cost

Date _____

I spent money on the following:

Item	My reason to purchase	Cost

Date _____

I spent money on the following:

Item	My reason to purchase	Cost

Date _____

I spent money on the following:

Item	My reason to purchase	Cost

Date _____

I spent money on the following:

Item	My reason to purchase	Cost

Date _____

I spent money on the following:

Item	My reason to purchase	Cost

Date _____

I spent money on the following:

Item	My reason to purchase	Cost

Date _____

I spent money on the following:

Item	My reason to purchase	Cost

Date _____

I spent money on the following:

Item	My reason to purchase	Cost

Date _____

I spent money on the following:

Item	My reason to purchase	Cost

Date _____

I spent money on the following:

Item	My reason to purchase	Cost

Date _____

I spent money on the following:

Item	My reason to purchase	Cost

Date _____

I spent money on the following:

Item	My reason to purchase	Cost

Date _____

I spent money on the following:

Item	My reason to purchase	Cost

Date _____

I spent money on the following:

Item	My reason to purchase	Cost

Date _____

I spent money on the following:

Item	My reason to purchase	Cost

Date _____

I spent money on the following:

Item	My reason to purchase	Cost

Date _____

I spent money on the following:

Item	My reason to purchase	Cost

Date _____

I spent money on the following:

Item	My reason to purchase	Cost

Date _____

I spent money on the following:

Item	My reason to purchase	Cost

Date _____

I spent money on the following:

Item	My reason to purchase	Cost

Date _____

I spent money on the following:

Item	My reason to purchase	Cost

Date _____

I spent money on the following:

Item	My reason to purchase	Cost

Date _____

I spent money on the following:

Item	My reason to purchase	Cost

Date _____

I spent money on the following:

Item	My reason to purchase	Cost

Date _____

I spent money on the following:

Item	My reason to purchase	Cost

Date _____

I spent money on the following:

Item	My reason to purchase	Cost

Date _____

I spent money on the following:

Item	My reason to purchase	Cost

The End

To keep track of your finances you will need a financial plan. The plan will indicate your income you make and expenses you incur. The plan will need to be setup and maintained on a regular basis.

There are many sites which you go to which will have samples of financial plans you can download for free. If not you can easy put one together quickly with information from sites.

Conclusion

I have provided some guidance for you to reduce your debts and create some wealth. You need to take action for this to work and do not be disappointed with any setbacks as this is common.

You need to always stay in control of your finances and your spending habits.

Remember in all things to take control of your life while enjoying family and friends.

.